"It Is My Love," I Embraced It; Frustration

Ezra 4:4-5

Then the people of the land weakened the hands of the people of Judah, and troubled them in building, and hired counselors against them, to frustrate their purpose, all the days of Cyrus king of Persia, even until the reign of Darius king of Persia. *(American Standard Version)*

Apostle Sheba Brown

Apostle Sheba Brown is a native of Albany, New Yo
She was ordained as an Apostle November 15, 2008
She is submitted under the covering of Chief Apostl
Ken Moses and Apostle Adelicia Moses. She is a
motivational speaker and life coach In addition to
overseeing several ministries, and counseling Pastor
across the country, she is an entrepreneur and the so
proprietor of Crown Twist & Tibbs Enterprise, locat
in Albany, NY which is the headquarters to five other businesses tha
operate under her entrepreneurship. God has anointed her not only to
bring change and order to the body of Christ, but she is also a woman
who will go behind the veil to receive the direction of the Lord for H
people. She operates in an anointing in the Apostolic, Prophetic and
Deliverance Ministry.

2 Samuel 22:31 Your way is perfect, Lord, and your word is correct. Yo are a shield for those who run to you for help. (African American versi

The Plan Of Frustration Has Been Crushed

The wolf is lurking; "Yes, the Wolf of Frustration." It is so unfortunate when the enemy uses one of the most common methods of the kingdom of darkness to prevail against the righteous. The begrudging attitude of the righteous causes us a defeat when frustration is on the scene. There is a certain attitude we must take against frustration in order to overcome its plan. Frustration's plan is to annoy and torment you while you are ang with feelings of efforts being nullified. Frustration is the attitude of a perso that stops one from fulfilling, progressing, and succeeding. One who lose their ability to control a feeling that is purposed to thrust you into an unac complished defeated place.

No man or woman of God should be defeated because of irritation or having been irked by another person's behavior. Frustration should not b allowed to cause a person to become wearisome because of their own disappointment or because of others who disappoint you. Arrest the plan of the enemy, control your agitation, irritation, being irked and move forward by prevailing against the enemy. Upon this rock I should Build my Church and the Gates of Hell shall not Prevail against it.
Don't let Frustration Prevail, Arrest the Assignment.

$15.99

Dedicated

I dedicate my book to my son Stanley Brown Oliver for choosing the book cover design. This book is written out of my personal deliverance from the works of the flesh; "Frustration". I had to close the doors of the demonic therefore the kingdom of darkness was overthrown by the word of God, the Blood of the Lamb, and my testimony.

To my closest friend, I thank God that he picked Ingrid K. Bennett to write a chapter in my book. "The Cave of Your Emotions" is written by Ingrid K. Bennett. The revelation that God gave to her in this chapter is phenomenal as she continues to write chapters in some of my other books. I hope that this will inspire her to launch some of her own books. I thank you Ingrid K. Bennett for your obedience and your constant encouragement.

IT IS MY LOVE. I EMBRACED IT; FRUSTRATION

EZRA 4: 4-5

"Then the people of the land weakened the hands of the people of Judah, and troubled them in building, and hired counselors against them, to frustrate their purpose, all the days of Cyrus king of Persia, even until the reign of Darius king of Persia". (American Standard Version)

Apostle Sheba Brown

ISBN 978-1-304-80641-3 copyright 2013 by Lulu publishing

ISBN 978-1-304-03543-1 copyright 2013 by Lulu publishing
Content ID: 13854488

Printed in the United States of America.

Lulu Enterprises
3101 Hillsborough Street
Raleigh, NC 27607

THE CAVE OF YOUR EMOTIONS

Chapter Written By Ingrid K. Williams

I was inspired to write this chapter after overcoming the hidden devices of frustration and the cunning strategy of frustration that the enemy uses to move the people of God away from their assignment. I want to thank Apostle Sheba Brown for the opportunity to write a chapter in her book because it has been an inspiration.

The Cave of Your Emotions

==

========================

Frustration: "a feeling of anger or annoyance caused by being unable to do something: the state of being frustrated"[1] [1] Merriam-Webster Dictionary

Frustration is the feeling of being sad and upset or annoyed because of the inability to achieve your goals or God's Assignment. When you are frustrated you are overrun with emotions, including fear, depression, aggravation, upset, anger, loneliness and abandonment. All of these emotions are a lie and when left unchecked and unchallenged you will believe what you feel and forget or ignore what you know about the word of God.

Frustration will cause the person to run and hide in the caves of their emotions. Caves are caverns that have formed inside a cliff or a mountain. They are dark and cold and the further you go into a cave the darker and colder it can become. When frustrated instead of standing like a mountain, unmovable and abounding in the works of the Lord the person is left believing that they are inadequate in fulfilling their God-ordained mandate.

1 Corinthians 15:58 "*Therefore, my beloved brethren, be firm (steadfast), immovable, always abounding in the work of the Lord [always being superior, excelling, doing more than enough in the service of the Lord], knowing and being continually aware that your labor in the Lord is not futile [it is never wasted or to no purpose].*" (Amplified Bible) When in the midst of a circumstance, trial or assault by the enemy we tend to crawl into our emotions and languish there hiding, but mostly hiding from

whatever is inside the cave of our emotions. Spiritually, we find ourselves standing on the outside of the word of God because we are not successful in completing the mandated assignment due to the fact that we are frustrated.

When frustrated we will seek to hide ourselves from the accountability to the word of God and rest in the dark places of our emotions and there we will stay until we walk out or we are carried out. However, if you're not careful frustration will be allowed to thrive and you will die in the cave of your emotions and with this death your anointing, your destiny, your purpose, your assignment, your mandate and the will of God for your life will die also. Moreover, the death of your assignment can have a devastating impact on the people who are assigned to you. People may be delayed in fulfilling the will of God for their own lives because you allowed frustration to prevail.

If you do not leave the cave of your emotional frustration you may not be able to recover God's original assignment that God assigned to you. How many have walked away from their assignment, or backslid never to recover and left themselves in a state of being broken always? The shell of your former self or just a skeleton can only be identified by the garments of righteousness that was once worn and when you were in your God ordain assignment. In the natural, how many skeletons have been discovered and could only be identified as royalty because of the symbols of their heritage, their robe, scepter, crown, or ring.

If in this state, they, that is the Body of Christ that find you say, unless God raises you again dead you will remain for only God can raise the dead. People cannot raise you from your depression, frustration, bitterness, or your inability to overcome frustration. If anything they are well equipped to make you more depressed, and more frustrated. People cannot raise you from your aggravation. If anything people are well able to make you more aggravated toward yourself and your leader. People cannot raise your ministry again.

If left up to them you will never return to your assignment. If anything they are well suited to make sure your ministry remains dead. But God's word can quicken the dead which is why God will send someone to remind us of the word of God according to Romans 10: 14 which declares, *"But how are people to call upon Him Whom they have not believed [in Whom they have no faith, on Whom they have no reliance]? And how are they to believe in Him [adhere to, trust in, and rely upon Him] of Whom they have never heard? And how are they to hear without a preacher?"* (Amplified Bible)

Looking at the scripture we find that the Prophets of Israel were hunted and killed by Ahab and Jezebel. 100 prophets were hidden in caves by Obadiah, a strategically placed agent of the Lord who feared the Lord and served as the Governor of Ahab's house – 1 Kings 18:4 *"For when Jezebel cut off the prophets of the Lord, Obadiah took a hundred prophets and hid them by fifties in a cave and fed them with bread and water"(Amplified Bible).* One prophet, Elijah the Tishbite, was not hiding in the caves with these prophets that were hid by Obadiah.

Yet, Elijah himself was not hiding at this time. However, in time Elijah the Tishbite demoted himself from being a bold Ambassador and Mouthpiece for the Kingdom of God to hiding in a cave because of his frustration believing there were no one left that loved God other than him and that Jezebel desired his life also. Elijah is known in scripture for the great victory he had won on Mount Carmel. Just like some of us we were known of our authority to slay the enemy.

1 Kings 18: 37-40

37 Hear me, O Lord, hear me, that this people may know that You, the Lord, are God, and have turned their hearts back [to You].

38 Then the fire of the Lord fell and consumed the burnt sacrifice and the wood and the stones and the dust, and also licked up the water that was in the trench.

39 When all the people saw it, they fell on their faces and they said, The Lord, He is God! The Lord, He is God!

40 And Elijah said, Seize the prophets of Baal; let not one escape. They seized them, and Elijah brought them down to the brook Kishon, and [as God's law required] slew them there (Amplified Bible).

Jezebel threatened his life, as enemies do, and he ran from the enemy, as the righteous should not do. Why did he run? Elijah had just achieved a public victory by the hand of the Lord in the face of a bold enemy. His victory was all the more dynamic because it demonstrated who God was in the lives of His people and who God is against Elijah's enemies. But his greatest victory was in the previous chapter *1 King 18 when he obeyed the living God who commanded Elijah to show his face to Ahab that day after being in hiding for three years because Ahab and Jezebel were killing the prophets – 1 Kings 18 1-2 "[1] After many days, the word of the Lord came to Elijah in the third year, saying, Go, show yourself to Ahab, and I will send rain upon the earth. [2] So Elijah went to show himself to Ahab. Now the famine was severe in Samaria (Amplified Bible).*

Elijah's obedience led to a face to face meeting with Ahab. It was a clash between titans one a keen ambassador of the kingdom of God and the other the husband to a shrewd ambassador of the kingdom of darkness. Obedience to God activated Elijah's anointing which declared the enemy's defeat openly, mocked the enemy, prevailed against the enemy and led the nation of Israel to assume their authority by slaughtering the 450 false prophets at Elijah's command. Elijah's assignment was complete. His obedience led to a national victory. Indeed, his obedience to God allowed him to be courageous because Elijah was led by the spirit of the Lord instead of his emotions.

A whole nation was under siege by an unchecked enemy until one man of God heard God and followed what God told him to do. God did not ask Elijah to meet with his emotions to see if they were in agreement with the Lord's instructions. Whatever emotions Elijah had they did not stop him from executing his instructions from the Lord. Elijah began his assignment on Mount Carmel as a man who was not frustrated by the assignment or in the assignment and consequently the enemy was scattered.

Now the enemy is in an uproar. Jezebel threatened Elijah and Elijah packed his bags and left town 1 *Kings 19:*

3 "So let the gods do to me, and more also, if I make not thy life as the life of one of them by tomorrow about this time"(Amplified Bible). I wonder why Elijah didn't tell Jezebel by this time tomorrow she would be like her false prophets that fell under the sword of the Lord. Elijah had much to say in the previous chapter and he stood with a God who enforced everything he had to say but now frustration is his assignment. Threatening the enemy and believing God for your victory and the victory of the people is a farfetched thought when you are having a frustration pity party.

Yes, frustration breeds fear and fear births church runaways. A runaway is one who leaves God's assignment for their own agenda. Elijah was solid in his victory. We know he no longer felt secure in his authority because he stopped operating in his assignment but his assignment included Israel – its men, its women, its children, their property, their places of worship and more. He walked away from the people God charged him to protect. Frustration will do that! It will cause you to leave the people you were assigned to serve because being sensitive to the spirit of the Lord is no longer your concern.

The enemy wasn't just coming after Elijah but all that were attached to him. Frustration will cause you to run away from your wife, your husband, your children, your leader, and your congregation. Frustration makes you vulnerable to the enemy! Who would now intercede? Who would now declare? Who would now charge the angelic host to take the head of the enemy off on behalf of Gods people? Who? While God can raise another to be his servant God had chosen Elijah to be his servant for such a time as this. But Elijah allowed his frustration to submit to his emotions and he ran away into the wilderness.

1 King 19: 1Ki 19:4 " But he himself went a day's journey into the wilderness, and came and sat down under a juniper tree: and he requested for himself that he might die; and said, It is enough; now, O LORD, take away my life; for I am not better than my father's" (Amplified Bible). The cave of our frustrated emotions can include several feelings such as:

- DEPRESSION
- AVOIDANCE
- BLAME
- INSENSITIVE TO GOD'S PURPOSE AND CALL
- HOPELESSNESS
- CARNALLY MINDEDNESS
- SHORT SIGHTEDNESS
- TIMIDITY
- LACK OF FAITH
- ANGER

Many times when we run away from our assignment frustration, disappointment, and unresolved issues can cause us to question the stability of church and God's Word. God has assigned us to venture without a map or a spiritual compass. Unfortunately, We run away hoping we will be fed at the next church and we stumble into in our self-imposed wilderness journey. It is hard to find a person in the wilderness that's why people run there. Like Adam and Eve they ran their too. Where was Elijah going? *Jeremiah 23:24 " Can anyone hide himself in secret places so that I cannot see him? says the Lord. Do not I fill heaven and earth? says the Lord" (Amplified Bible).*

Here we are frustrated by the enemy's attached assignment. What Elijah failed or forgot to consider was he was anointed for this diabolical force of evil. When he ran, the scriptures say Elijah ran 80 miles away out of the jurisdiction of Ahab and Jezebel *1 King 19: 3 "Then he was afraid and arose and went for his life and came to Beersheba of Judah [over eighty miles, and out of Jezebel's realm] and left his servant there" (Amplified Bible).* The immature do that you know – they travel long distances to avoid being accountable. Now in the cave of his emotions the Lord asks Elijah why are you here? Here we have God who created the heavens and earth and all that dwell in it. Here we have God that could raise the dead and a nation.

Now Elijah out of breath and strength is running in the wrong direction and the Lord would say, "Why are you here man of God and who told you to lodge in a cave when I the Lord commanded you to fight the battle of the enemy? Who told you to ask for death? When I the Lord told you to bring and end to the threats of the enemy? What have you allowed to drive you to the cave of your emotions? Was it not fear, frustration, and despair?"

Now Elijah's emotional frustration had the best of him. God was not in his frustration, anger, discouragement or in him having a moment. Why are you here Elijah? No wonder he became weary in fighting with the enemy. He used all of strength to run away. Elijah is collapsing and complaining of his discouragement. God sat Elijah up, fed and gave him water because his journey was long. Can you see Elijah at the mouth of the Cave staring in the direction he just came from with the 1000 mile stare after the Lord

told him to go and anoint *1 King 19: 15-17*

[17] *And the Lord said to him, Go, return on your way to the Wilderness of Damascus; and when you arrive, anoint Hazael to be king over Syria.*

[16] *And anoint Jehu son of Nimshi to be king over Israel, and anoint Elisha son of Shaphat of Abel-meholah to be prophet in your place.*

[17] *And him who escapes from the sword of* [a] *Hazael Jehu shall slay, and him who escapes the sword of Jehu Elisha shall slay (Amplified Bible). It was his frustration that gave Elijah strength to run away. Humility and repentance will be needed to regain strength to turn back to fulfill his God given assignment.* Chapter written by Ingrid K. Williams

NOTES

NOTES

The Wolf Is Lurking

Psalms 34:19 the Lord's people may suffer a lot, but he will always bring them safely through. (Africa American Version)

The wolf is lurking. "Yes, the Wolf of Frustration." Are you guilty or innocent of being frustrated ? It is so unfortunate when the enemy uses one of the most common methods of the kingdom of darkness to prevail against the righteous. Frustration is purposed to open up doorway to the demonic. The begrudging attitude of the righteous causes a defeat when frustration is on the scene. There is a certain attitude we must take against frustration in order to overcome its plan. One of the attributes of frustration is the inability to walk away with an understanding versus walking away feeling irked. One thing about frustration is its sole purpose is to make sure that a person leaves the conversation angry.

The Bible said be angry but sin not. Unfortunately we go beyond being angry because it is more important to us to prove our point then to decide to leave with an understanding. Frustration's plan is to annoy and torment you while you are angry with feelings of efforts being nullified. Frustration is the attitude of a person that stops one from fulfilling, progressing, and succeeding. A person that is frustrated can lose their ability to control a feeling that is purposed to thrust you into an unaccomplished and defeated place.

No man or woman of God should be defeated because of irritation or having been irked by another person's behavior, conversation, or action. Frustration should not be allowed to cause a person to become wearisome because of their own disappointment or because of others who disappoint them. Arrest the plan of the enemy and control your agitation, irritation, being irked and move forward.

Jesus said, *"Upon this Rock I should Build my Church and the Gates of Hell shall not Prevail against it"*. Don't let frustration prevail arrest it.

NOTES

NOTES

I Am The Parent

==================================

=====================

Don't you agree the wisdom of a parent conflicts with the wisdom of a teenager? Will the parents just say "Amen!" Just as the wisdom of a parent conflicts with the wisdom of a teenager so doesn't the wisdom of a leader conflicts with the wisdom of a member. Both positions are on entirely different levels of wisdom, understanding, and warfare. Just as the teenager is not sensitive to the parent when the parents have their best interest so is a member insensitive to the leader when the leader has their best interest. When a child becomes frustrated with the parent they run away from home. When a member becomes frustrated with their leader the member runs away from the church. Do yourself a favor and stop being frustrated. Understand when frustration is on the scene most of the time you will see self-pity, rejection, despair, and a broken heart. Yet, frustration is purposed to cause us to be in an abnormal state of perpetual grief. Hurts bruises the senses. The feeling of being rejected causes one to be loaded with heaviness. *Isaiah 61:3 Says, to appoint unto them that mourn in Zion, to give unto them beauty for ashes, the oil of joy for morning, the garment of praise for the spirit of heaviness;*

My point must be made the person said! How can I make my point while running ? Why run unless I agree with frustration having its perfect work. Running has a purpose you know! The purpose of a teenager running away from home is to prove their point to their parent just like that of a member. What's interesting is the member will go to another church and run from that church also trying to prove their point. "Oh No, there they go again; to another church! Frustration drives the member out of that church too. Before you know it the person is not attending any church or is now becoming the pastor of their own church. Oh don't forget the teenager who is running away and is staying with a friend that agrees with him. Although he isn't speaking to his parents; frustration in the end keeps him from speaking with those he loves and cares about. I wonder if he has even considered this. According to *Numbers 11:11-15 Moses prayed and said, "I am your servant, Lord, so why are you doing this to me? What have I done to deserve this? You've made me responsible for these people,*

12 they are not my children. You told me to nurse them along and to carry them to the land you promised their ancestors.

13 they are whining to me, but where can I get meat for them?

14 this job is too much for me. How can I take care of all these people by myself?

15 if this is the way you're going to treat me, just kill me now and in my miserable life! (African-American version)

Moses prayed and he said, "Lord why has thou afflicted thy leader have I not found favor in your sight that the burden of the people is upon me." Frustration births burdens, heaviness, and the feeling of wanting to give up. What Moses was really saying was I don't want to run away from my assignment; I don't want to give up on your people although I have now become frustrated myself.

It's difficult dealing with your frustration and the frustration of other people. Because Moses reached out to God he was able to overcome his frustration.

Like Moses, why don't you reach out to God? No one can hear you when you're running you must stop and talk about why you are frustrated. Are you guilty of being frustrated? If you said yes to this question ask yourself, "Why should I be frustrated when I could have gotten an understanding". Once God spoke to Moses and he was able to understand how to deal with the people and their frustration then they were able to move forward. Don't let frustration get you stuck. Remember those that were stuck wandered for 40 years in their frustration.

NOTES

NOTES

I'm Being Watched

==================================

======================

People don't watch the enemy or the sheep as close as they watched the shepherd. The shepherds are watched like a hawk and every mistake is recorded. Just like the teenager watch their parents like a hawk and recording every mistake but they don't watch their friends as close as they watch the mistakes of their parents. They will say something to their parents like, "When I was younger you weren't there and when I was younger you didn't come to my baseball game and when I was younger you didn't give me the gift I wanted for Christmas." But they never say to their friends when we were younger and in high school you slept with the love of my life. Neither do they say when I was in high school you told the teacher that I cheated. The mistakes of their friends were forgotten, overlooked, and never brought up. Frustration has a target against order, accountability and to those that are accountable to the kingdom of God. I don't know about you I will only operate according to God's word not according to the members, not according to friendships or children.

Frustration never allows you to see the responsibility and accountability of others, parents, husbands, wives, or leaders. The parent's position is that they went to work 40+ hours a week to pay the bills which was more important to them than the $399.00 X-Box for Christmas. The parent had to choose the decision of accountability of keeping a roof over your head or playing the X-Box in a homeless shelter. Although the parent is frustrated they continue to do what will give victory to the household by keeping their head up while doing the right thing that is more responsible. The parent was there when you had a fever and a cold and Tylenol and Cough Syrup was dispensed. The teenager's frustration gives the parent no credit for their accounts. Just like the member they expect everything from the shepherd and they become frustrated when there expectations are not met. It's important to consider that the pastor has 100 expectations on their desk yet a decision has to be made based on the word of God. Frustration breaks the relationship between the member and shepherd. The shepherd is saying I prayed for healing when you were sick, I prayed for your family members, I prayed for your children too. All of the shepherd's mistakes are recorded but none of the shepherd's efforts was notated. Just like the teenager with the parents. Are you guilty? Did frustration prevail and you are now on the run?

NOTES

NOTES

Frustrated At The Hands Of The Enemy

Judges 16

King James Version (KJV)

16 Then went Samson to Gaza, and saw there an harlot, and went in unto her.

2 *And it was told the Gazites, saying, Samson is come hither. And they compassed him in, and laid wait for him all night in the gate of the city, and were quiet all the night, saying, In the morning, when it is day, we shall kill him.*

3 *And Samson lay till midnight, and arose at midnight, and took the doors of the gate of the city, and the two posts, and went away with them, bar and all, and put them upon his shoulders, and carried them up to the top of an hill that is before Hebron.*

4 *And it came to pass afterward, that he loved a woman in the valley of Sorek, whose name was Delilah.*

5 *And the lords of the Philistines came up unto her, and said unto her, Entice him, and see wherein his great strength lieth, and by what means we may prevail against him, that we may bind him to afflict him; and we will give thee every one of us eleven hundred pieces of silver.*

6 *And Delilah said to Samson, Tell me, I pray thee, wherein thy great strength lieth, and wherewith thou mightest be bound to afflict thee.*

7 And Samson said unto her, If they bind me with seven green withs that were never dried, then shall I be weak, and be as another man.

8 Then the lords of the Philistines brought up to her seven green withs which had not been dried, and she bound him with them.

9 Now there were men lying in wait, abiding with her in the chamber. And she said unto him, The Philistines be upon thee, Samson. And he brake the withs, as a thread of tow is broken when it toucheth the fire. So his strength was not known.

10 And Delilah said unto Samson, Behold, thou hast mocked me, and told me lies: now tell me, I pray thee, wherewith thou mightest be bound.

11 And he said unto her, If they bind me fast with new ropes that never were occupied, then shall I be weak, and be as another man.

12 Delilah therefore took new ropes, and bound him therewith, and said unto him, The Philistines be upon thee, Samson. And there were liers in wait abiding in the chamber. And he brake them from off his arms like a thread.

13 And Delilah said unto Samson, Hitherto thou hast mocked me, and told me lies: tell me wherewith thou mightest be bound. And he said unto her, If thou weavest the seven locks of my head with the web.

14 And she fastened it with the pin, and said unto him, The Philistines be upon thee, Samson. And he awaked out of his sleep, and went away with the pin of the beam, and with the web.

[15] *And she said unto him, How canst thou say, I love thee, when thine heart is not with me? thou hast mocked me these three times, and hast not told me wherein thy great strength lieth.*

[16] *And it came to pass, when she pressed him daily with her words, and urged him, so that his soul was vexed unto death;*

[17] *That he told her all his heart, and said unto her, There hath not come a razor upon mine head; for I have been a Nazarite unto God from my mother's womb: if I be shaven, then my strength will go from me, and I shall become weak, and be like any other man.*

[18] *And when Delilah saw that he had told her all his heart, she sent and called for the lords of the Philistines, saying, Come up this once, for he hath shewed me all his heart. Then the lords of the Philistines came up unto her, and brought money in their hand.*

[19] *And she made him sleep upon her knees; and she called for a man, and she caused him to shave off the seven locks of his head; and she began to afflict him, and his strength went from him.*

[20] *And she said, The Philistines be upon thee, Samson. And he awoke out of his sleep, and said, I will go out as at other times before, and shake myself. And he wist not that the LORD was departed from him.*

21 But the Philistines took him, and put out his eyes, and brought him down to Gaza, and bound him with fetters of brass; and he did grind in the prison house.

22 Howbeit the hair of his head began to grow again after he was shaven.

23 Then the lords of the Philistines gathered them together for to offer a great sacrifice unto Dagon their god, and to rejoice: for they said, Our god hath delivered Samson our enemy into our hand.

24 And when the people saw him, they praised their god: for they said, Our god hath delivered into our hands our enemy, and the destroyer of our country, which slew many of us.

25 And it came to pass, when their hearts were merry, that they said, Call for Samson, that he may make us sport. And they called for Samson out of the prison house; and he made them sport: and they set him between the pillars.

26 And Samson said unto the lad that held him by the hand, Suffer me that I may feel the pillars whereupon the house standeth, that I may lean upon them.

27 Now the house was full of men and women; and all the lords of the Philistines were there; and there were upon the roof about three thousand men and women, that beheld while Samson made sport.

28 And Samson called unto the LORD, and said, O Lord God, remember me, I pray thee, and strengthen me, I pray thee, only this once, O God, that I may be at once avenged of the Philistines for my two eyes.

29 And Samson took hold of the two middle pillars upon which the house stood, and on which it was borne up, of the one with his right hand, and of the other with his left.

30 And Samson said, Let me die with the Philistines. And he bowed himself with all his might; and the house fell upon the lords, and upon all the people that were therein. So the dead which he slew at his death were more than they which he slew in his life.

31 Then his brethren and all the house of his father came down, and took him, and brought him up, and buried him between Zorah and Eshtaol in the buryingplace of Manoah his father. And he judged Israel twenty years.

Frustration was the open door to Samson's emotionalism. Samson's ministry was called from his mother's womb by the angels of God to come forth as a judge to Israel. Yet trying to fulfill his ministry assignment Samson found himself at the door of frustration most of the time. His emotionalism was a constant battle against him walking in the victories of God. After coming through yet another battle he was set up by the enemy and here comes the Delilah. Frustration will almost mark a victory concerning Samson's ministry.

From the beginning the instructions from God was that Samson shouldn't cut his hair because he was called to be a Nazirite. Samson blindsided by his emotional frustration and his desire to have it his own way caused him to be snared by the trap of Delilah. Frustration will serve you; are you guilty? Well let justice according to the word of God prevail and take frustration down by getting back into the obedience of God as Samson did. Samson never did get an understanding until the end. He allowed himself to become frustrated but he never allowed himself to have an understanding concerning this fact; all frustration had to do was keep him tied up with the trickery of Delilah. The enemy, the devil, the adversary was going to fight him for the Win. How? By keeping him from fulfilling his assignment as God's judge to Gods people. Interestingly, how we blame the husbands, wives, church members, and leaders even the president of the United States is being blamed for people's frustration.

What happened to us putting the blame in the right place? The blame belongs in the Enemy's Camp. Frustration is just another cunning strategy that the enemy uses to overcome those of us that are operating in our mandate. Our mandate is the assignment that God has trusted us to fulfill. When frustration arrives victories don't happen. Let's be honest frustration is preventing us from fulfilling the plan of God for our lives and the lives of others that we are to touch. The greater enemy that fights against us is the enemy of our frustrated emotions.

When our emotions are frustrated we operate in the attributes of the devil. What are the attributes of the devil? No just balance, being out of order, becoming liars, sowers of discord, gossipers, slanders, cunning, wicked, and having no godly principles. If you see these watch out frustration is lurking! When our emotions become frustrated we lose immediately. For a certain amount of time a child needed the concern of their mother. Although once the child got to a certain age they believe that they will no longer have need of the concern of their mother.

The purpose of the previous statement is for the reader to understand that the leader must always have a concern for the member even as the parent will always have a concern for their child. Many may say that this would not be the truth but how can we say that God will not have a concern about us even though we don't want him to. the leader needs someone to be assigned to them as they are assigned to the people.

Just like Aaron was assigned and concerned about Moses while he was concerned about the people. In all honesty rather you are frustrated, disappointed, feel mistreated, let down or being yelled at it doesn't change your assignment to your leader, it doesn't change the leaders assignment to you and it doesn't change the parents assignment to their child.

Neither does it change God's responsibility to us all. This is why he sent Jesus! It's a "Hard pill to swallow Huh?" Do you think the all knowing God didn't know that we would betray the Kingdom and him? Yet, he sent Jesus still. This is the reason why we must not allow frustration to prevail.

NOTES

NOTES

Frustration Criticizes

==================================

======================

Frustration would allow you to believe that others have a disgusting attitude toward you and that their cold in their hearts toward you. The weapon of frustration operates by allowing you to believe that no one has a concern that you are feeling rejected or that you have feelings of being put off. Understand this that wherever there is frustration there's going to be the spirit of trickery, the spirit of perversion, manipulation and deception.

Frustration will leave you without an understanding and the lack of understanding in the end will leave you in a lonely and defeated place. Are you guilty of being frustrated? Yet, frustration opens doorways to the demonic. We all understand that wherever there is a perverse spirit it will cause one to err in every good work like a drunken man staggering. Therefore, frustration would cause us if we're not careful to do that which is convenient or comfortable. Yes the unnatural; This is when God steps out of the way and allow your will to move in. Romans 1:28 Frustration will also allow us to know where we are in our righteousness especially when we are operating in perverted practices like frustration.

Furthermore, it makes the situation more difficult for you if you are not strong in the word of God. You can be defeated by the assignment of frustration because it is so cunning. Frustration will cause you to be out of control. It will cause you to put yourself in the fire of the enemy by being directed by your emotions and not by the will of God and his Word.

Frustration will cause you to break a promise, your word, it will cause you to be unfaithful, not to mention uninvolved and disconnected. Frustration will make you forget the days of Greatness and Success. Frustration is an open door that will orchestrate a demonic world wind twirling through the cycles of failure and cycles of disappointments… Frustration will put you under the enemy's control by destroying your own assignment. It is a viral infraction in the Body of Christ purpose to disturb ones rest, promotes stress, and bring anxiety by causing health problems, mental distress and chronic oppression.

When operating in these tools of the enemy God's plan and your assignment will be held up. Get your tools off the table that the Lord has prepared before you in the presence of your enemies. Frustration will fight to prevail. Frustration causes you to decrease instead of increasing in the will of God properly. Frustration blindsides your ability to discern what is happening in God's next move for you. Samson was another one frustrated in his assignment therefore never accomplishing fully what God wanted him to accomplish.

He assassinated the plan of God based on feelings of being dismissed, discouraged and frailty. Fortunately, Samson regained his passion in his last hour when things were at the final stage. Standing between two pillars and taking control over frustration had caused him to be successful in completing his assignment. Even if you feel like you're at the end of your rope you still need to take control over your frustration. When a person is having feelings of being defeated frustration along with heaviness causes the person to resign from submission.

Are you guilty of letting frustration win? It is impossible to submit to God when you are frustrated.

Stop running with no destination in mind. Before you can even get to alter your decision frustration will fight to take over. Arrest the assignment of frustration, failure, defeat, embarrassment, and dissatisfaction by picking up God's weapons. We are called to bind up setbacks take the limits off. Fight for growth and continue to move forward. *Psalms 34:18 declares, "The Lord is there to rescue all who are discouraged and have given up hope."(African American)*

NOTES

NOTES

www.ingramcontent.com/pod-product-compliance
Ingram Content Group UK Ltd.
Pitfield, Milton Keynes, MK11 3LW, UK
UKHW041839200726
13854UKWH00003BA/1221